Bleed Between The Lines

Stephanie Farrell Moore

blood
moon
POETRY

Cover illustration by Christabel Blackburn
ISBN: 978-1-7399155-4-4
Imprint: blood moon POETRY

For my body, my boys and all those who bleed

x

Note from the Editor

When I look back over all the notes I've written for our poetry books in my position as Editor-in-chief of blood moon POETRY, I realise they have all started in very similar ways. I talk about what it's like for women in the world today, how we have come so far yet not nearly far enough. We are not yet ALL safe. We are not yet ALL treated equally. We are not yet ALL free from oppression. We are not yet ALL heard.

blood moon POETRY was established in 2020 with the mission to amplify women's voices through the publication of their words. *Bleed Between The Lines* is our fifth book and it comes hot on the heels of *Trigger Warning*; an anthology of poems written by women who have survived sexual assault and violence. We opened submissions after the murder of Sabina Nessa and were overwhelmed by the response from hundreds of women; their poems like diamonds waiting to be unearthed from the rubble of their experience at the hands of men.

We published two of Steph's poems in *Trigger Warning* because we all found her words to be both powerful and personal. She managed to bring her very raw feelings into the light without forcing us to read them, instead I felt as though she were both talking just to me and for every woman with her poetry. This is the magic of her work – the ability to conjure utterly familiar and beautiful imagery, while resisting over-whelming her readers.

The subtle majesty and feeling in Steph's poems are woven through every page of this book. Her passion for the practice of Menstrual Cycle Awareness is here, rippling through Winter when she speaks of rest. Rest. Such a loaded word for women and often the thing we crave the most. Her chapter on Spring is a quiet celebration of budding hope, the slow lifting of energy and growth that we must both savour and contain if we are to bleed peacefully later on. But it's in Summer that I find my home in Steph's words: the part of my own cycle that always finds me faltering, unable to feel my way through into Autumn without crashing. Her poems in this season are exalting, honest, risky. We can be ripe and ready right before the fall, and she doesn't shy away from holding those things together. Presenting them as the most natural of bedfellows – dark and light, rest and revival, full and fragile.

So what I find here is, of course, the very essence of womanhood. We are complex, multi-faceted and – if we can live by our cycles, honour our internal and ancient rhythms – we are powerful. When I read *Bleed Between The Lines*, I experience a collection of poems that has responded to a shift in consciousness that is taking place right now. Women are rediscovering their bodies, the beauty in our bleeding and the absolute control it can give us over how we care for ourselves and run our lives. **Not all women bleed**, but ALL women have been taught to deny their inner wisdom, silence their innate knowing and deafen themselves to their truth. Steph seeks to remind us that we all possess within us the power to live in sync with our bodies and for women - bleeding or not - that may mean saying no, resting and prioritising self care much more regularly. By publishing her poems, we hope to make *Bleed Between The Lines* a tool for education, empowerment and above all a way to help remove the shame around menstruation and reinstate the right language.

Society is still catching up, but this collection shows me that we ARE ripe. Ripe for change and the possibility that safety, equality, being heard all start with bringing those things home to our bodies.

Lunar Love,

Holly Ruskin
Editor-in-chief & co-founder
blood moon POETRY

Note from the Author

Bleed Between the Lines came to be during a prolonged period of ill health when I had no choice but to address my mental and physical health and make the healing of my body (and my relationship with it) a priority for what felt like the first time in my life. I've always been intrigued by the menstrual cycle and half-heartedly kept track of when my period was due but in the last couple of years it's become such an integral part of balancing my life, that most of the choices I make day to day stem from seeing life through the lens of the four phases of the menstrual cycle- our 'inner seasons'.

Menstrual cycle awareness has played a huge part in my recovery. It can get us out of our heads and into our bodies, helping us to be here now and, although I was pretty shit at meditating, when I randomly started 'talking' directly to my inner seasons as a way to connect with my body I felt a space open up and a new voice of truth and creativity come through. It was the quiet voice inside we don't always believe but that, during this dark time, I decided to start trusting. Over the course of a year I wrote what came up in those conversations with my body and decided to weave them into a collection as a reminder to myself and an offering to other women. I thought that by sharing my intimate experiences, I could play a small part in encouraging cycle-related discussion and normalise talking about our menstrual blood…the wonder and despair of our cyclical bodies. I would love to live in a world where asking 'what day are you on?' is as natural as 'how are you?'. To me, cycle check-ins are the opposite of small talk; an antidote to the superficial, scrolling tempo that eats away at our time and souls, giving us permission to acknowledge what's really going on in our beautiful, complicated bodies.

As a mother to two young sons growing up in a patriarchal world, it's important to me that they too have access to this knowledge. By talking about menstruation in all its bloody glory I hope to help them grow into men who understand more about the female experience. In turn, it's my hope that they will be able to respect and honour the women in their lives without feeling awkward or ill-equipped.

I'm currently training with Red School on the Menstrual Leadership

Programme and their revolutionary teachings have opened up an even deeper layer to my fascination with all things cycle-related. When we acknowledge that the menstrual cycle isn't just about the bleeding, yet this is the part most affected by our life choices, then we are liberated to make radical changes to the way we live. We can allow ourselves to rest, knowing we will absolutely reap the benefits later. Embracing slowness and stillness without guilt is fucking hard, but if we're willing to defy societal pressures and expectations our inner Winters can be the biggest invitation to surrender. I'd love women to reach for this collection when they need comfort for the difficult moments in the month and to know they are not mad in their inconsistencies and inability to be the same version of themselves every day.

Everyone's inner seasons are going to feel unique - there is no 'perfect cycle' - but, if you are a person that has periods, please use my words as a springboard for exploring the energy and rhythms of your own cycle more intimately. There are plenty of period and hormone self-help books out there but I hope Bleed Between the Lines will connect with you on a deeper level, helping you to remember the magic of something that your body already knows.

I approached Holly at blood moon POETRY press (aside from the appropriateness of the name!) because I knew her fierce love of women's words and desire to amplify the wrongfully shamed, silenced parts of the female experience would give my womb-born poems a perfect platform to exist safely, boldly and in a way that would reach the people that need and want to read them. I am so grateful to have collaborated with her and the rest of the blood moon team on this intimate collection.

Love,

Steph x

Contents

Foreword

Even though half of the population on this planet will, at some point in their lives, have a menstrual cycle, it is sadly still a taboo topic in much of day-to-day life. Luckily, we are living in a time where Menstruality is coming out of the shadows, and it is people like Stephanie who are helping to shine a light on it. At Red School, we believe that the power held within the menstrual cycle can create profound transformation in people's lives and Bleed Between the Lines beautifully captures the depth and versatility of this experience.

Stephanie holds your hand as she takes you through the inner seasons of the menstrual cycle, exploring the humbling and empowering emotions that come with each one, with a rawness and realness that makes her poetry effortless to connect to.

In the inner winter, she explores the deep connection to the inner-self, the curiosity and beauty of menstrual blood and the deep release we can feel when we let the outer-world go. In inner spring, the curious emergence of returning into the world and the tenderness that comes with that. In inner summer, the heat, the fullness, the true embodiment of self and of pleasure. And in inner autumn, the fierceness of emotion, the deep call back to earth, as we begin to move inwards once again.

To those on the edge of discovering the depth of their own menstrual cycle, let Stephanie's poetry be the map to guide you deeper. And to those who are already well aware of the beauty and power of menstruality, you will close the final page feeling like you have come home to yourself once again. Stephanie's vast experience and wisdom of her own menstrual cycle shines through every word in this collection - it is truly medicine for these times.

Alexandra Pope and Sjanie Hugo Wurlitzer, co-founders of Red School and co-authors of *Wild Power: discover the magic of the menstrual cycle and awaken the feminine path to power*.

Reading our Inner Seasons

For more in-depth knowledge on the inner seasons Wild Power by Alexandra Pope and Sjanie Hugo Wurlitzer has all the incredible cyclical wisdom you could wish for. As a starting point here is an outline to use as a guide for navigating this collection (all days are approximations because every woman is a unique cyclical being!):

Winter: Day 1-5 **Menstruation**. From the first to the last day of your period. The time for solitude, rest and listening to your deeper longings and the call of your purpose. Do less and keep your diary empty where possible. While you're letting go of your blood, release anything else that's weighing you down.

Spring: Day 6-14 **Pre ovulatory/Follicular phase**. Energies start to rise. A time for exploration, discovery and going gently. A rebirth. The inner child in you takes delight in play and curiosity. Plant the seed of possibility for the month ahead.

Summer: Day 14-20 **Ovulatory phase**. Pleasure seeking and a time for expanding into the full expression of yourself. Socialising and communicating come more naturally. More balance. Able to deal with work and life and engage with the needs of others as well as your own.

Autumn: Day 21-28+ **Pre-Menstrual/Luteal phase**. Let go and slow down. A time to listen to what is important and for saying no to things that don't align with your truth. More rest, more reflection and grounding. Sit with discomfort in your life and listen to what it's asking of you. Time to speak out in the face of bullshit and perfect the power of NO!

Years of not wanting to bleed
to never be seen with
a tampon up your sleeve
globs of blood on toilet seats
told not a decent excuse
to miss out on PE
and now I dream of
blood-soaked knickers
rescued by my inner winter
the chance to give in
to the reverent whispers
they convinced us
weren't worth giving a shit about
not meant to find out
or sit still for long enough
to acknowledge the red magic
that simply exists within us
without ever having to lift a finger.

WINTER

When
I tug gently
pull out my cup
filled up
with deepest red
my beautiful blood
a distillation
of a difficult month
I wonder
I hope
this tender hurt
is filtered through
with enough
unconditional
self-love.

Over
four weeks
you cushion
my womb
making room
for the most
precious seed
of truth
illuminating
sacred intelligence
that radiates
from furthest away
and on the months
no life
comes to stay
you pave the way
to make changes
the saving grace of
twelve times a year
being able to
break down
and start again.

So sensitive
at the best of times
then you
remove my leaves
leave me naked and
exposed
to the elements
and it literally feels
like I'm bleeding
raw soul
from my whole body
till I actually bleed
she is here
and only then
the sweetest relief

I'm home.

You
made her
do things
she didn't
want to do
pushed her
to push
through
moved her
too far
from view
and now
it's her turn
to tell you
what
not
to do.

The storm
won't hit you
if you're already
lying down
the invitation of
winter's welcome
willing you to rest
sit this one out
listen to the gale
the howl
snapping branches
asking you to
detach
detach
detach
no action needed
allow the bleeding
to be your healing

lie back.

My insides
coming out
now is
the moment
to tell them
all the ways
our bodies
have been
wronged
the call of
this pain
in the depth
of our core
a fond
too warm
reminder
to surrender -
it's time
to come home.

Relishing
in squelching
all the blemished
rotting, rotten leaves
deep into scrubland
means
unburdening myself
of the month's leftovers
transforming
the many little deaths
of me
into something holy.

Align
with the tilt
of your axis
the world
doesn't resist
the setting sun
switch off your light
don't look outside
for lightbulb moments
that won't hold the answer
hold your womb
stop pushing through
till tomorrow
or tomorrow will be
exactly the same
except you'll
fade earlier
missing
the subtlety
of the way.

In the bareness
of winter
I will not decorate
my branches for you
hanging blankly
for good reason
my season's greetings
after all those
twinkling lights
the bright gold and glitter
trimmed with lace and
favourable behaviour
I am not here
to look pretty
I am here to be
stripped bare
taking care
but not caring
a week of safety
in dark red
plainness
is the only thing
that will save me.

She is gone
and I
mourn
the safety
of retreat
I get from
bleeding
a feeling of
not needing to
be seen
turning my back
on being needed
and I know
tomorrow
I'll be
called back
out to the
wild

no more
hiding
for a while.

SPRING

April showers
do whatever the
Fuck
they like
no such thing
as a warning.

That
darkest energy
under her seabed
becoming
potent wonder
for re-discovering
her electric orange
current

Womb
hanging
empty
too soon
for new heights
can you be
weighed down
by lightness?
porous to
the dust of
every idea
pummelled
by wind and
sea spray
this sharp tongue
eroded

I know
my imperfect texture
is only one version
of wearing
this lifetime.

The space
in her womb
leaves   r o o m
for truth

Returned.

with   space   in   my   bones

)hollow(

in the best way
my blood outside of me
a deep room for seeking.

In the springs

after
I didn't rest
or listen
to my winter

I'm dragging
my existence
with me

indifferent
even to the
things
that usually
bring me
purpose and
pleasure.

When I meditate
on the feeling of
spring
I see two hands
holding mine
gently guiding
me back
into the light

takes a while
to adjust my eyes
to the brightness
but a voice
that sounds
like mine says

there's time.

This spring
bring your
inconsistencies
and radical brilliance

dare to
stop
listening to a world
that burdens you
with an ambition
to show up
as this tame, cloned
version of yourself
day in
day out

erase the doubt

you are brave enough
to let
the wilder ones
OUT.

It's not a perfect sunrise
that makes birds sing
it's simply the light

find a way to
turn *towards* it
now is not
your time to
carry what is **dark.**

She is
always has been
the too early pink cherry blossom
on show before she's ready
sprung too soon
none of us ever knowing
how cold
or over-exposed she still feels and
what a *performance* it all is
holding on to those branches
oh, so tightly
before the warm breeze
steals her petals
regret disguised
in the froth of confetti.

A spoonful of youth
the tease of
hide and seek
tipping towards
bursts of deliciousness
mixed
with the temptation
to stay
completely   (hidden)

can you trust

exposing

this softest skin?
don't pick your fruits before
travelling the whole
e   x   p   a   n   s   e
of you.

Break out of your
own captivity
end the lamenting

make way for
beautiful change

SUMMER

I am QUEEN
the best kind of greedy
worst thoughts can't
touch me
on the verge of
ferocious
tempted by
the salty
waves of pleasure
breaking into regret
if I don't rein her in.

.

I am here
to remind you
how good
your body feels
sink your teeth
hungrily
into the truth
of what moves you
it's almost like
it will always be
impossible to ever
be *too full*
your fullness
all yours to savour
expanding into
the present
oh so able
to be generous
without resentment.

Some wild flowers
can self-seed
in rough walls or
hazardous cracks
in the road
so don't think
you can't survive
in the *tiniest* of gaps
between your darkness.

It's like paradise
overnight
everything is
happening at once
and it's now that
you take it
in your stride
not worrying
about pleasing
or politeness
no fight to feel
seen
no desire to
fit in
flitting and
flickering
entirely uninhibited
licked by the
rays of the sun.

As the heat rises
                 your roar travels
                                  further
the wildest of
offerings
a red hot wish
to always
be this
unstoppable.

Ovulation

all she can taste
is love
in all its forms
turned on
by not
holding on
the temptation
of filling days
to the brim with
one hot day
melting into
another
but then
the come down
s
   i
n
   k
ing
into
ripened ground.

We ignore
nature's clock
the rising and
setting sun
strong pull
of the tide
patterns in
the stars
and magic
in the moon
but still
this womb
holding out hope
for new life

heaving herself
out towards
enlightenment.

Leaning into forbidden
carrying the raw ache
of every Eve
smirking at the thought
that any Adam
could ever dampen
this desire
that runs deeper
than these physical bodies.

Stroll
this summer path
as if for the very first time
the high of last month
is not for chasing
savour
the crushed berries
running down your chin
only
now
is for licking

Preoccupied
with nectar-seeking
high on self-belief
effortlessly achieving
by now
you have
the reassurance
a green canopy
of leaves
for protection
shading you
from the
searing heat.

She is the
caterpillar
caught in
digesting itself
from the inside out
this mush of
wet pulp
just a twisted
crumple of flesh
turned wild with
vibrations
waiting...
stuck in the
anticipation of
wings.

So light
I frighten myself
threatening to
evaporate
I say
a prayer
please
remember this
perfection
when you tip
over the edge
into extinction.

AUTUMN

Scorched
by the crossover
crumbled
into autumn
and I ought
to sit in

stillness

feel the twinge
of my lining
release
r e l a x
the muscles that
hold on
to the stories
entangled in
this month's suffering
let go
let flow
slowly
slower
more and more
still
more.

On day 21
I turn in on myself
desperate to
barricade doors
ignore the world
blacken blinds
clutch time
to my hot lumpy chest
and tell everyone
I'm busy
sorry I'm busy
for the next…

well
for the foreseeable
while I long
for the belonging
of my bleed.

Overnight
my colours turn
the ends
of my nerves
cut   off
without warning
the goodness I'd found
in recent days
past its best
left with the choice:
carry on digging
for 'normal' or
disconnect and
reject the external
sink into
acceptance and
just become
one with the
wallowing.

Autumn jars
mainly because
letting others
down
while we hold

S P A C E

for ourselves
has been
frowned upon
forever
and so
we carry on
until our bodies

S H O U T

by making
themselves
a burden.

The reason
I don't want to be seen
on the page
or I manage to
put it off
for days
is because of
the discomfort
that lies in wait
the weight of
welcoming change
dredging up words
that don't want
to be moved
upended
they'd rather stay

          suspended

in the comfort
of keeping things
as they were.

Caught in the
trap of my
wrongness
almost every time
I'm pre-menstrual
there's the
shameful thought
I want to be dead
tormented by
the desperation for stillness
and darkness
and nothingness
until I smell
the end of autumn
in the air
that whiff of decay
a way for
me to hold
on for spring.

Womb
soon to be emptied
but while
the bowl
in my hips
is full
I use the power
of my stillness
to listen
for magic stored
from the month
before
she knows
what's pure gold
and what
just needs to *go*.

Just before
the bareness of winter
whipped into a frenzy
gale force unrelenting
branches bow and bend
defenceless in the storm
threatening to break
can't keep up with
what I'm dropping
every thought
project
object
tossed aside
at the tiniest sign
of something shinier
mind excruciating
trying to find
what?
I don't know
(will I ever know)
what I'm looking for?

I crave winter
when everything
stops existing

including me
bare trees
leafless
heart open
womb
bleeding.

The tiniest hint
she's about to
bring red winter
my heart sings
pink strip
of discharge
my sign
of encouragement
not long
till I can
stick a pin
in my bloating
pants soaked
body and heart opening
halting
further mental
damage.

Why is it
that some months
you hold onto my blood
muddying me
with thoughts
of if I'm pregnant
or not
bloated with
the heavy load
of 28 days' worth of woes
won't you hurry up
unburden me
unfurl into trust
remember how to
love
and stop
hurting?

About blood moon POETRY

blood moon POETRY is a small indie press and a home for poetry written by women from all walks of life. Born from a desire to find and nurture talent that would otherwise go unheard, we specialise in the compilation, editing and publication of collections centred on themes of womanhood. Our bi-annual digital journal also features work from our online community of female poets, authors and illustrators from around the world. In seeking out new and undiscovered creative women, our mission is to amplify their voices to ensure we are the place where women can be heard above the noise.

Connect with us on Instagram @bloodmoonpoetrypress and Twitter @bloodmoonpoetry
Find us and subscribe at www.bloodmoonpoetry.com

Other titles from blood moon POETRY

Faces of Womanhood Edited by Holly Ruskin
A collection of poems about womanhood written by female poets, this anthology is an exploration of what it means to be a woman. Featuring the words of 50 women, Faces of Womanhood is the journey to and from contemporary womanhood. Faces, places and ages are explored in ways unique to each woman and poet. Their work captures and (momentarily) pins down the 21st century mother, sister, wife and daughter, so that this collection can be read as a timeless study and celebration of our differing experiences. A book that draws together voices from all walks of life, Faces of Womanhood is the perfect place to meet yourself, the women you have known and are yet to discover.

This Skin I'm In by Ebony Gilbert
This Skin I'm In is a vulnerable exploration of what it means to be a woman living in a body - her body, and surviving with it through trauma, shame and addiction. A full frontal and an excavation of the soul, each poem is a love letter written by the author to herself and any woman who has ever felt the loneliness and pain of survival. They are also a declaration of tenacity and victory written by a mother, sister, friend and little girl. This is not just a collection of poems but a handbook for survivors.

Silver Hare Tales by Lauren Thomas
Silver Hare Tales is a journey through the author's family history; it's the retelling of ancestral stories and the charting of a return to her womanhood. It speaks to the idea of a woman's longing for where she came from. The lands that birthed our mother's mothers; smells and sounds just tangible as we cross the line between sleep and dream. Grounded in truth, warmth and emotion this book is a treat to heat your bones and a reminder to all women that our strength lies in being rooted.

Trigger Warning Edited by Holly Ruskin &
Guest Edited by Chloe Grace Laws
Trigger Warning is a unique collection of poems written by an array of women who have chosen to share their experiences of sexual assault and violence. Moving and incredibly powerful, each piece is cathartic.

Women's experiences have been shut down and belittled for too long; these stories tell us so much about the urgent work that must be done to make every one of us feel safe. Every woman who contributed to this collection has shown vulnerability and courage - it is a rallying cry for change that all should listen to. More than a book of poems, this important publication brings out into the light what is so often left for women to carry in the darkness.

All available in paperback on Amazon. To purchase visit our website www.bloodmoonpoetry.com/print

Lightning Source UK Ltd.
Milton Keynes UK
UKHW041558131222
413865UK00004B/136